Jennifer L. Rogala

Illustrated by Jacob Nicholas

"When My Nose Runs Where Does It Go?" by Jennifer L. Rogala. ISBN 1-58939-866-1.

Illustrated by Jacob Nicholas.

Published 2006 by Virtualbookworm.com Publishing Inc., P.O. Box 9949, College Station, TX 77842, US. ã2006, Jennifer L. Rogala. All rights reserved. No part of this publication may be reproduced, stored in a retrieval system, or transmitted in any form or by any means, electronic, mechanical, recording or otherwise, without the prior written permission of Jennifer L. Rogala.

Manufactured in the United States of America.

For Samantha and Jillian

When my nose runs where does it go?

Can the foot of a bed wear a shoe?

Can my eardrum be played in the half-time show?

Can the teeth of a comb ever chew?

Does the mouth of a river eat noodles?

Can the eye of a needle look?

Can my Dad's Adam's apple be used to make strudel?

Can my hangnail be used as a hook?

Can the tongue in my shoe lick an ice cream?

Is a riverbank wealthy and rich?

Can the bridge of my nose span across a small stream?

Does a potato's skin ever itch?

Are hives on my skin homes for bees?

Would a palm tree ever wear gloves?

How can my skin crawl when
it has no hands and no knees?

Can an artichoke's heart
ever love?

Can my armpit be inside a peach?

Can a head of lettuce think?

Can a wave in my hair ever crash on a beach?

Can a trashcan lid ever blink?

Can the pupils of my eyes go to school?

Can a kneecap be worn on my head?

Does the crown of my head have diamonds and jewels?

Can somebody sleep on my nail bed?

Can a lock of my hair bolt a door?

Can the legs of a table run?

When my foot falls asleep
does it dream, drool, and snore?
Can my funny bone
really have fun?

Can my eyelashes be part of a whip?

Can my hips be the fruit of a rose?

Can my chest hold a treasure in a sunken ship?
How can my feet smell if they don't have a nose?

Will the calf of my leg ever moo?
Does this neck of the woods have a throat?

Can my rib cage be found in a circus or zoo? Can my belly button fasten my coat?

Does the nose of a plane ever sneeze?

Can the arms of a chair give a hug?

Can my hamstring be served on a sandwich with cheese?

Can the shoulder of a road ever shrug?

Can an ear of corn
hear sounds and words?

Can my voice box be
wrapped with a bow?

Are my goose bumps related to web-footed birds?
Can the iris of my eye bloom and grow?

Can I unlock a door with piano keys?

Can I weigh myself with fish scales?

Can a traffic jam be served with crumpets and tea?

Can a coin nod its head and wag its tail?

Can a two-story house tell tales?

Can my eyeball be used to play catch?

Can I build a house
with a hammer and toenails?
Do chicken pox lay eggs
that will hatch?

All of these questions are silly.
I'm just having some fun with you.

Goosebumps are pimples on your skin when you're chilly.
A needle's eye is what you put thread through.

Your nose cannot run
in a road race.

But I think that you
already knew.

Your nose has no legs and it's attached to your face.
When it runs all you need is a tissue.